The Wise Man Stories

Friends Anonymous

ISBN: 0-87516-371-8

Published by
DeVorss & Company
Box 550, Marina del Rey, Calif. 90291

Dedicated to our daughters Aileen Hohmann and Elaine Bush and their families.

May, 1978

INTRODUCING . . . .

In the far-flung reaches of Eternity, the Decision was made. The Wise Man would visit the earth, and mingle with the people.

He chose to live in a little house on the edge of a small village, near the forest. Simple yet profound was to be his life and teaching.

Blessed is the community that receives and entertains the Wise One. Fortunate is the individual who embraces and understands the message of the Wise Man.

THE PATH to the door of the Wise Man was well worn.

The curious came. All they saw was an old man in a cabin, and wondered.

The puzzled ones came, and experienced an unraveling of their difficulties.

The inwardly lazy came and asked for exact answers. They found none but were stirred from their lethargy to seek meanings.

The children came and found in the story-telling and nature-loving man an introduction to the greatness of life and the beauty of existence.

The worldly-wise looked for his diploma, but he had none to show. No words were heard, for the Wise Man had none to offer.

Hungry ones came, knowing they would be fed. When fortune changed, they returned with arms full.

In the evening, the Wise Man looked at the path, well worn with footsteps and smiled. His rest was peaceful.

IT IS IMPORTANT to realize that life is ever new; that there is no duplication. Similarities, yes; identicals, no; patterns, yes; sameness, no; rhythm, yes; repetition, no.

THE MAN spoke to the Wise Man:

"I am full of fear. The deep tragedies and troubles that visit others, the calamities, the illnesses, the heart-aches—just thinking about them happening to me scares me. This is not a fanciful problem, Wise Man; it is very real to me."

Quietly they sat for a while; then the Wise Man said:

"Each man's trouble is individual, and comes to him with the strength to bear it. Life will not ask you to carry a load too heavy for your arms. I have talked with many who have problems and have yet to find one without the inner strength to bear his burden. You see the catastrophe, but you do not know the inner capacity."

The easy, somewhat uneventful life of the man suddenly included a deep and difficult problem. He did not flee, panic, run away, refuse, or try to escape, but looked for that inward strength—and found it. Fear had been replaced with the awareness that comes with understanding.

He would have thanked the Wise Man, but he was gone.

"**H**E DID NOT give me advice, which I would have welcomed, but I felt inspired."

"And I went with a question, but he did not answer; however, I was helped."

"He asked me to return later and, when I returned, my problem had been solved."

"He came to me, for I refused to visit him. And he helped me."

"He assisted me physically, for I am crippled. He had little to say, but his actions were rhythmic, beautiful, and direct."

They shared their experiences, and each one knew he received that which was needed.

THE YOUNG man approached the Wise Man:

"It seems to me that I have more than my share of accidents. I tend to stumble into the catastrophes of life to a much greater extent than others. When we are picking berries, it is I who am stung by the bees; I am the one who stepped on the snake in our path; I was drawn into the whirlpool and nearly drowned; it was my hand that was burned when I reached for the hot handle at the picnic. Am I really prone to these situations and can they be avoided?"

The Wise Man smiled:

"There is no force that is pushing you into these incidents. One simple statement will make plain the situations that come to you. You are out of harmony with the conditions that exist.

You need to acquire what has been called the 'dignified pause'. For you are going just a little faster than conditions warrant. It would be well to commence your day with a period of pause. And then, before every event, sense an actual stoppage within time, in which you pause and stop your rushing for a brief moment. This moment will add the dimension of awareness so that you do not speed too quickly into events without a certain measure of what might be called foreknowledge. At first the attitude of the 'dignified pause' can be practiced, deliberately installed into your living method, purposely observed. In time, the response will be automatic and it will occur without your attention. Why not give it a try?''

There were no more stories of accidents or near accidents about the young man.

No SINCERE cry for help ever goes unheard.

S HE WAS known for her many kind deeds. One day she came to the Wise Man.

"I really have a problem. For the first time I feel that someone is taking advantage of me. You know the invalid who lives at the end of Main Street. I have been at her beck and call for many years, and her demands have, in my estimation, become excessive. And yet I cannot discontinue my services. What shall I do?"

The Wise Man said:

"For true service, there are two definite requirements: the need, and, secondly, love to do the service. Both must be real and not assumed or pretended, else the service is incomplete or becomes merely movement in time. Need is of course varied and not merely physical. There are deep inward needs, yes, even needs born of boredom. But if another serves out of compulsion that must and cannot refrain from doing, or from a thought of a reward or benefit to the server, then the action is not entirely complete. Certainly good may result from it, but not the very best that is possible. That is the sum total of service, but its application is not easy. Find out exactly what is occurring and you will have your answer.''

In a short time, the woman knew.

THE WISE MAN was addressing the group:

"Learning is slow; meaningful learning has not the speed of a flying arrow. But the experiences that come to each one of you contain the precious gem. Seek it; endeavor to comprehend the reason for the situation which you confront, whether joyous or accompanied with sadness—and in seeking the meaning, endeavor to by-pass the ego, the big self, the conceited 'I'."

It seemed to those in attendance as if the words were meant for each one individually. And yet, after the session, when those present compared notes, the same remarks were translated and comprehended differently. It was as if each one had been addressed personally and had not heard the words intended for the others in attendance. But the significance in the lives of all present became intense and much heaviness was lifted.

The physical presence of the Wise Man was gone, but his influence lingered.

TRUE FREEDOM is an inward state. It does not depend on outward circumstances. The man most free may be in bonds; the greatest slave may live in a servanted mansion.

THE YOUNG MAN approached the Wise Man.

"How can I know myself?"

Long the Wise Man looked on the youth. Fnally he broke the silence and said:

"You are defending your limitations."

Defending limitations?! Yes, he was. And as he watched his actions, partial enlightenment reached him. The Wise Man had spoken true.

After many months, the youth met the Wise Man again:

"I no longer excuse my limitations nor defend them, but I yet do not feel that I know myself."

Again the Wise Man pondered long. Then he said:

"You are blinding yourself with your ideals."

Ideals are blinding?! It took long for the boy to accept himself. And in accepting, in the full responding to himself, without the excuse or the defense, and without the blinding, he found the gem of Reality, the spark within, that portion which is eternal, buried deep below all the debris of the mental mind, to the level of spirit—and he knew himself.

When he met the Wise Man, they merely shook hands, sat together without words, and enjoyed the communication.

THERE SEEMED to be no inspiration for continuing the poetry. She had secluded herself in her room repeatedly, working hard to continue her method of expression. Finally she looked up the Wise Man.

"Poems are not made—they are born," said the Wise Man. "Live fully and you cannot help but express."

The poet had her answer.

THEY KNOCKED at his door, loudly. And then they walked away.

"He must be gone," they said.

Early the next morning, he opened the door, stretched, and welcomed the day.

One of the men returned.

"Why didn't you answer our knock last night?"

"Oh, did you knock?" queried the Wise Man. "I wonder why I didn't waken? Sounds different from the usual echoes of the woods generally awaken me. All I can say is that probably I could not be of help to you."

The man said:

"Well, strangely enough, the solution came, and we no longer have a problem."

"How far can I trust intuition?" he asked.

"Understand intuition," said the Wise Man, "for intuition is the faculty that tells you where to land your feet after you have taken the leap. It is that which tells you when to turn when you are running. It is action within an action, and action within the immediate moment. Consequently, it becomes the activity beyond the mental planning and deliberation. Intuition never takes advantage of another person. True intuition can be trusted."

The man pondered long on the words of the Wise Man. He realized that much he called intuition was merely his own thinking process in action and was not the extra ingredient described by the Wise Man. He admitted that he, who felt he possessed an exceptional amount of intuition, was instead glorifying self acts and deliberate manipulations under the guise of intuition.

Several months later, the two met again. The Wise Man looked deeply into the eyes of the other, then said:

"You have now sharpened and purified the tool of intuition."

"Oh—but," said the man, "there has been no occasion since I spoke to you for intuition to work."

The Wise Man responded:

"But now you know; before you only thought you knew."

And the Wise Man was gone.

"**B**UT I CANNOT live without him,''
said the weeping widow.

The Wise Man said:

"Life leaves no vacuums. You do
not need to try to 'cram' the emptiness
which you feel. A substitute may mo-
mentarily weary you to a place of for-
getfulness, but this does not satisfy the
emptiness. Permit, do not hinder life
when it offers the intended. For life
does not continue as a vacuum; you
will see.''

No words spoken by others, though
in kindness and with good intent,
quieted the sadness and enabled the
continuance of living, as the words of
the Wise Man. A new interest was
awakened. What would life offer? How
would this that seemed like a vacuum
be filled? What new form of living

would be presented if she allowed it to unfold?

It would have been her delight to tell the Wise Man how wonderfully her life developed. But when she looked for him, he was gone.

THE WISE MAN was well aware of the extent of influence which he exerted over the village. He was extremely careful in using this power. Well he knew that dependency upon another, or reliance or insistence upon the judgment of someone other than himself, can be weakening to man. And he saw the same principle working in reference to the little village.

The townspeople often found the Wise Man absent. He would be gone for weeks. And often it seemed to them that the trips were gauged to include those times when important decisions had to be made by the populace. And yet they were aware of the influence of his presence, and found themselves pondering and deciding in accordance with the basic ideas of life as taught by him.

The Wise Man loved the village, and the villagers loved the Wise Man. But neither robbed strength from the other, or made dependency a part of the structure. Learning was direct, and the teaching enabled the weak to find inner strength and the strong to use their strength properly.

POTENTIALS ARE sharpened by use, not by discussion.

T HE MAN approached the Wise Man.
"I have no problems. I live to myself alone."

The Wise Man searched for meaning, and said:

"Man solves problems—or man creates problems." He turned and walked away.

"What could he mean by that?" thought the young man. "My carefree, unresponsive and deliberately unimportant existence—I have no problems to solve, and what kind of problems might I be creating for others?"

They met again. This time the man was weary from effort expended in earning that which he took from life, pulling his share of the load, and finding a measure of opportunity for service to others.

"I am full of problems now, but for the first time I feel alive, useful, and in the flow of life itself."

The Wise Man smiled. The clay was throbbing with life.

ENTHUSIASM WITHOUT zealotry; appreciation without attachment—these are the evidences of balance.

"REMARKABLE MAN," said the stranger who passed through the country and heard of him.

"Remarkable person," said the resident of the town, acquainted with incidents in which the Wise Man had been involved.

"Remarkable teaching," said the student who had carefully scrutinized his remarks.

"Life in this world is remarkable," said the truly enlightened one, who had been influenced and affected directly by the visitation of the Wise Man.

The Wise Man listened, heard the comments and realized that the depth and extent of his service was limited.

THE YOUNG man was rather flippant.
"But this little defect in my character is not serious; I am hurting no one and it won't hurt me. Why should I make an effort to change and drop this habit?"

The Wise Man said to the youth:

"I see a hole in the elbow of your sweater." The boy looked and noted the hole, turned to the Wise Man, but he was gone.

The young man had his answer.

THE YOUNG man poured out his agony to the Wise Man:

"My dreams are shattered. My education, so dearly bought by my parents is wasted. My future is bleak and uncertain."

His words were mere whispers, for an ailment of the throat had robbed him of his voice. And all his energies had been aimed at the goal of becoming an orator. He had a message, he felt; a message that the world could well use. And, he was aware that the gift of speech and his pleasant personality had a profound effect on his hearers. And now all was lost.

The Wise Man looked long at the young man and felt the pain of the loss. Then he said:

"But, young man, look at what you have left. Your hands are powerful—why not employ them to present the truth you have for the world?"

And now the books of the young man, whose voice is entirely silenced, are spread among many people. The Wise Man visits the thinker often, and they find conversation unnecessary as they communicate in the silence. And the young man knows that his message has reached a multitude—more than his voice could have found. And others have picked up the brand and carried the torch of the message.

THE APPLAUSE continued. The room was filled with the sound of clapping hands that would not be silenced. Once more the curtains parted, and the girl with the instrument played another composition, lifting the hearts and minds of the hearers, transferring the sounds from the strings of her instrument and finding an echoing response. For music is the eloquent tone of Truth, especially when presented by the fingers of talent with humility. The room was tingling with appreciation of the offering of the gift by the talented young lady.

Near the back of the hall sat the woman, adding a note of discord to the scene. Jealousy, envy, and deep anger prevented her from receiving the beneficial flow from the music being presented. So engrossed was she in her own troubles that she was unable to benefit from the solacing and healing quality of the good music. For a long time her thoughts were so far away from her immediate present that she scarcely heard the tones. Her first awareness of the scene around her, made her feel a repugnance toward the enthusiasm the audience was showing.

"Why, they are acting like fools," she said to herself, "it seems as if they have lost their dignity—standing up to clap for that girl's performance."

The scene changed. The group was leaving the building. The woman found herself walking beside the Wise Man. He turned to her and said:

"Did you hear the concert?"

"Why, of course; I was there, wasn't I?"

Silently the Wise Man walked a few steps, then turned to the woman:

"Did you hear the concert?"

"Well, I think I heard it; I was there."

They walked out of the door and into the street, and once again the Wise Man said:

"Did you hear the concert?"

And suddenly the woman knew and understood. The burden of her antagonism, her envy, her jealousy, left. The sounds unheard in the concert hall returned from the pages of memory and, although not forceful and fully defined, nevertheless accomplished the healing touch so often given by the hearing and understanding of inspired music. She walked down the road in ecstacy. She turned to try to explain to the Wise Man that after all, she had heard the concert. But the Wise Man was gone.

WHEN THE Wise Man entered the home, he sensed the rhythmic vibration of harmony and love. The evening was spent in happy conversation and companionship and comradeship that delighted all present.

The woman in the wheelchair remarked:

"We owe so much to your teaching, oh Wise Man. You found me bitter, antagonistic, blaming God for the accident, miserable and most unhappy. But you taught the better way, and life has become not only tolerable, not only acceptable, but also a fulfillment. There is meaning, there is purpose, there is a sense of vitality and satisfaction unsuspected. You, Wise Man, showed us the Truth. I am beginning to understand the usefulness of the accident and the pain that has been my portion. There is a service performed for me by life itself in permitting the accident, for truly a greater life has unfolded, not only for me, but for others in our home.''

The Wise Man uttered:

''Some pains on earth refuse to be relieved. Greater than the pain is the discovery of acceptance.''

When the Wise Man left, the love and peace and contentment seemed intensified.

THE MAN met the Wise Man on the street.

"Let us go in and eat," he said.

When they found a quiet booth, he spoke:

"Why do you waste your life, Wise Man? All you have is the little house at the edge of the woods. You could amass much money, for you have persuasive powers and could rule men. Look at me—I have made a fortune, my family is wealthy. I have education and learning. I am a powerful man. Get smart— consider what I tell you, and make something of your life."

"I will consider," said the Wise Man. And they parted.

Years passed. Once again the two met on the street. The Wise Man said:

"Let us go in and eat."

And when they found the quiet booth, the man spoke:

"God has been unfair to me. He has visited me with great adversity. My wife proved unfaithful; my children neglect me shamefully; my wealth has not brought me the satisfaction that I expected. Even my friends have little use for me. You have your hut by the beautiful woods and your garden gives you much good food. Did I put my values in the wrong places? Could it be that I placed my security on my own efforts, my own wisdom, my own smartness, my own cleverness? Maybe, after all, you have been the wise one. I will consider what you have taught me. But I now realize that you have said nothing. How have you taught me without eloquence or persuasion?"

The two parted. The Wise Man returned to his hut near the forest and raised his heart in gratitude with the songs of the birds in the trees and was grateful indeed to the God he served. He knew true peace.

THE COUPLE quarreled with indignation and bitterness, with many sarcastic and degrading remarks. Soon, however, the sharpness of the tone was lessened, and the two involved held hands and appeared to be peaceful.

They turned to the Wise Man:

"You see, Wise Man, there is a benefit to this quarreling. It is only a surface storm. We can find the depths of peace way down deep inside. Don't worry about us."

The Wise Man said:

"Careful be that the storms do not race shoreward, where the depths cannot be found."

And the Wise Man was gone.

THE MOTHER was deeply troubled.

"I am worried about my son. He seems so different from others in the family. He prefers his own company; his interest is in books and reading, to the exclusion of other activities. Furthermore, he is not physically strong. How will he ever get along in this life? How can he make a living? He won't listen to me. What will become of him?"

The Wise Man quietly answered the woman:

"Greater than your son's problem is the worry you are holding. Here is the real arena of operation. For you are hurting yourself at the same time as you are confusing your son. Worry robs you and makes of you an individual who cannot help another."

"Not even once have I looked at my worry or considered it to be a problem. In fact, isn't it my duty as a mother to feel great concern for my children?"

The Wise Man's eyes twinkled.

"Now we are facing the problem. You are, are you not, slightly enjoying this feeling of worry?"

The woman's face showed a startled look, then anger, and then a question, and finally a light and smile came to the features.

"No wonder they call you the Wise Man," said the woman. "I suddenly recognize that I have been proud of a negative attitude. Perhaps now I can help my son instead of condemning him. Thank you for showing me myself."

Two women, neighbors, were busily discussing affairs when the Wise Man walked by. The conversation abruptly stopped. He greeted them courteously and proceeded on his way.

"I wonder if the Wise Man would help us?" said one. Their eyes met and suddenly they knew the injustice which they were planning, the concern to build their reputations at the expense of another, the applause they were seeking at the cost of another's sacrifice.

The two women parted without a further word, each in her own thoughts. And the Wise Man knew, and smiled.

MAN IS BORN TO LEARN. The amassing of knowledge is indeed part of the learning process, but there are lessons not contained in textbooks, which are acquired through experiences, relationship with others and the full living of life.

THE TWO men, close friends, were sitting on a log in the forest, watching the day silently flow into the evening. The sounds of the forest became stilled, and were being replaced with the night noises that, to the listening ear, are quite as alive and present as the sounds of the day.

"I have wondered, Wise Man, why in some instances you speak so generally to some people and so specifically to others. You at times give definite instructions for persons to follow, while in other instances you seem to ignore the problem and speak in generalities. And yet the results are contained well in the contacts you make. People continue to come to you and go away refreshed."

"It is difficult to describe and talk about methods," said the Wise Man, "because in truth I do not find that I follow any specific system. In fact, I would rather not even try to repeat a previous teaching. I find it hard to explain exactly how or what happens. I sort of open my being to Truth, to what really is, and try to recognize what is occurring beyond the expressed words of my visitor. To know one's true need is not easy.

"And no two people have the same problems, in reality, for every circumstance is somewhat different. So I am not groping in my mind for an answer based on previous answers, but trying to comprehend the immediate without reference to the past. It seems awkward to speak of this, but I find it somewhat fascinating to organize my thinking and really observe myself. All of this is unconscious; I do not deliberately think of casting out the past, even, but that obviously is what I do.''

"Could you teach another to do the same?'' asked his friend.

"No, I don't think so," said the Wise One, "because it is not a method. It is not a routine form of operation. In fact, it is definitely the absence of such, and movement within the immediate seems to me to be of vital importance. And teachings of exact methods could bind and corral the inspiration of the immediate moment. At least that is how it seems now to me.''

"I am your friend. People have come to me too with their problems and questions. I have tried to hand out the instructions as you have given them to others, but somehow it has been a stumbling experience and not really conducive to real help. Now I know why. I am serving stale food and a cold broth. I will not attempt to mimic any more.''

THE TWO young boys were full of vitality and strength.

The race was about to begin. The Wise Man took the hands of both boys and he said:

"Good luck to you."

When the contest ended, the loser came to the Wise Man:

"You wished me luck but I did not win."

The Wise Man looked at the lad and said:

"Sometimes to lose is to win. The very best that can happen to you, at times, is not to beat your comrade. When you have put forth your best effort, you have won, even if another has excelled. If you learn this truth now, you will by-pass many greater difficulties as an adult. And you can actually delight in another's gain.''

"But I wanted to win,"said the boy.

"Yes, of course, but the trying and the doing is far more important that the final result,'' said the Wise Man.

The lad left, but his eyes were downcast, and he was kicking a stone before him along the path. It was obvious that he did not understand fully. But the seed was sown, and in the future events of life, the man may indeed taste the value of rightness rather than demanding the fruits of victory.

THE ARTIST poured out all the results of inspiration, the background of training, and the sum total of his inward feelings. Before him on the canvas appeared the scene that is beyond the scene itself.

Time passed. The painting was handed from man to man. There was a spark of response on the part of many. Finally it appeared on the wall of a castle, mixed with many objects of art and paintings of note.

The Wise Man was called for conference by the owner of the castle. He was in a dilemma and heard of a Wise Man who helped people. The troubled one poured out his problem, explaining in detail his concerns. The Wise Man listened without comment, then walked to the wall, faced the painting of Truth and said:

"What have you there?"

"Oh," said the troubled one, "I purchased that for much money—it is the work of a famous artist." The Wise Man turned:

"You have not answered my question." And he quietly left.

The puzzled one said to himself:

"What do I have here?"

For the first time he looked with seeing eyes at the masterpiece. And he found his answer.

THE WISE Man appeared in Townville. There resided a so-named Saint, full of good deeds and generous acts, admired by all.

The Wise Man was greeted by the Saint, embraced by him, and welcomed to his home. Many came to visit and explain the good deeds of the Saint. As the Saint listened with the Wise Man, he occasionally added details of his exploits, which might have been overlooked or forgotten by the story teller.

The Wise Man listened and listened. He smiled in benevolence, and occasionally frowned in dismay.

The next morning, the Saint began again to relate incidents to show his sainthood. The Wise Man turned and said:

"Where are You? I have heard of your exploits—but where are You? Where are YOU?" And he picked up his cloak, and suddenly he was gone.

Townville has changed. There is now no admired Saint. But there is a man, completely forgotten when his deed is accomplished, giving and blessing, spreading and witholding when required, and stirring Townville into its own strength rather than the worship of one man named Saint.

"I AM RUNNING away from home," said the lad. "I can no longer stand the bossing of my parents. I want some fun and a life of my own."

"Would you like to spend the first night in my cabin with me?" asked the Wise Man.

They talked of many things. The Wise Man spoke of inner urges and desires. The boy realized that it must be desire and not inner urge that was compelling him to leave his parents' home. They spoke of joy and peace and the boy realized that he was confusing fun with these necessary ingredients for fullness of living. They then spoke of stimulation and happiness, and the young man, in his search for happiness, began to wonder whether he was seeking the gratification that comes from stimulation, and missing true happiness.

In the morning, the boy rose early:

"I must go back and tell my dad not to hire another to fill my place in the family structure; I must ask my mother if she will set another plate at our table."

The Wise Man watched the lad walk down the path. The immediate crisis was over, he knew. He would meet the boy again, he was sure, for many questions were unanswered. But the direction of his feet was now correct.

THE DROUGHT in the land was severe. The man was vehement in his denunciation of God.

"God is unfair; He is unfaithful; He rejoices in man's misery; God is not good."

The Wise Man listened but said not a word. There are times when silence is eloquent, and argument would but feed the flame of anger.

Several years went by, and once again the Wise Man was in the vicinity of the drought-visited land. But now all was green and flourishing. He met the man again.

Haughtily and with great pride, he said:

"I am a success. I have amassed a great deal to myself. I have been wise in the way I have handled my life situ-

ation. Why, Wise Man, don't you con-
gratulate me?"

The Wise Man listened but said not
a word. There are times when silence
is more eloquent than speech, and
when words but add fuel to the flame
of a man's egotism.

And the Wise Man was gone.

SPEND NOT thy energies in comparing thyself with another, whether saint or sinner, but look within and find the strength to combat every tendency that does not spell progress.

"**M**Y SO-TERMED gift has been a constant source of distress," said the young man. "Because I have the capacity to express myself well, my parents, teachers and friends all recommend that I seek an outlet of teaching in the church. It is all heaviness to me, Wise Man, for I have no such leaning."

The Wise Man looked with pleasure on the young man:

"The highest path of expression differs for each individual. There is no one way that is best for all, and there is orderliness and a beautiful pattern when and if the individual can find the particular form of expression intended for him. Gifts indeed are precious, but only the person holding the Giver's treasure can know its proper usage.

Search within, young man, and listen to your inward urge.''

Some years later, the Wise Man traveled to a remote corner of the province. There, in a little schoolhouse, with five pupils, he found the man with the gift.

''I have found myself and my proper place in life, and I am deeply happy,'' said the man. ''Already six wonderful students have left and are serving and spreading knowledge. The five I am now teaching will find for themselves the places they can best fill. Some will be in public positions and others in less conspicuous situations. For your teaching has clarified much for me which I can transfer to these hungry-to-learn young ones. I know now that man must find himself before he can hope to be of real assistance to another.''

Yes, the family was disappointed, and insisted that their son had buried his talent. The townspeople droned on about the unrealized possibilities of one of their own. But the Recording Angel, dipping the pen in the ripples of Love, wrote many pages about the success of the man with the gift.

THE YOUNG man said:

"You know the feud that has existed between my clan and the neighboring town. The injustices visited by their forebears have been recited to me almost daily. I wonder, Wise Man, what is my proper attitude in this matter?"

The Wise Man said:

"Past history can be understood but cannot be changed. Inequalities of the past are not adjustable. Only the present is available to man."

The young man had his answer.

"WHY IS misery multiplied to my sister and her family?" queried the man. "It seems as if one catastrophe follows another—they no sooner overcome one massive difficulty than another presents itself. Now their son was killed by a falling tree—the boy on whom they looked with promise and delight."

"Your sister and the family know of a strength of which you are unaware. They entertain a faith in the Infinite that is greater than any circumstance. Faith in life and faith in eternity overshadows all the events that occur," said the Wise Man.

The brother responded:

"I must admit they ask for no sympathy, even in the midst of their most trying difficulties. Admittedly, there is a harmonious atmosphere in the home, and they seem to lack nothing. You may be right, Wise Man. My sister may, in reality, have more than the rest of us.''

The brother returned to his sister, not with pity, but with a willingness to learn, a request for understanding, and a hunger for knowledge of Truth. From the depth of experience, the knowledge of life itself, and an enduring confidence in the Eternal, the sister could fill the blanks and enrich the worldly-wise brother.

THE RAINS came early that year. The crop had not been completely harvested and, with the energy born of necessity, the townspeople joined the farm folk in the massive effort to precede the force of nature in its rampage. Early in the morning, all day, and late into the night, the Wise Man also worked in the fields, toiling with pleasure and rendering the service of his strength to the need of the moment.

The group assembled around the fire before retiring, enjoying the comfort that derives from a body tired and weary from honest toil. The Wise Man spoke softly, and imparted new energy with his words.

When the rains came in fury, the crops had been saved and the spirits of all were refreshed.

WHEN PRINCIPLES are known, details will fall into place without clutter. When structure is understood, the outward embellishments and trimmings are seen as such; any changes in outward appearance will not affect the structure. When basics are familiar, and foundations are comprehended, the observation of altered outward appearances destroys not the strength of the edifice.

THE YOUTH came to the Wise Man. "I am afraid to continue my education for fear it will rob me of my faith in the Supreme Being. My friends have returned from institutions of higher learning, devoid of belief in the Divine. I am not willing to sacrifice and give up my confidence and assurance in a God and a future."

The Wise Man looked with pleasure on the youth. "You need not fear knowledge. Man's mind as it searches uncovers seeming mysteries, all of which point to the greatness of the Divine One. Acquaintance with His creation leads to the Creator. The difficulty with man lies in his response to discovery, regarding it as his personal creation, rather than evidence of the Greater One, the Originator, the

Establisher. Whether you study the stretches of space, or reach into the miniatures of manifestation; if you ponder yourself or other humans, study animals, birds, or insects—no matter what field you choose, revelations disclose the Creator. Knowledge, rightly handled, can lead you to confidence, assurance, and greater respect for the wonders of His creation. Cherish true knowledge.''

The youth whistled as he walked the path from the Wise Man's cottage.

"I FEEL so utterly useless. Here I sit in the chair most of the day, unable to accomplish my work, and actually being a burden to my family. Why I am as useless as that big rock that I see out there on the edge of the field." The Wise Man listened, then turned his eyes to the window.

"I have often admired that rock to which you point. Once I saw a bird perch on it, and open its throat in glorious song. For many minutes I enjoyed its message. Look now at the setting sun and the beauty it imparts—the shadows it forms and the color it lends to that rock. Remember its service as a hiding place when the children play 'hide and seek'. Yes, I can see that rock serving. In the great economy of life, there is no surplus. And now I turn to you. How often have the children come to you for comfort; the youth have heard your advice and your counsel, knowing its truth even as they act out its denial; your influence is felt by distant friends as your fingers of prayer reach out to assist; you are serving by your need to be served. Useless?"

"I guess my God makes no mistakes after all," she was heard to say.

THE MAN said, "I have had a great life. Not only have I amassed wealth, but I have traveled much, learned a great deal, accomplished much. Only to you will I admit a great vacancy inside."

"Your addition is superb, but division you have not known," said the Wise Man.

"He must mean that I must share," the man said. He divided with his family, gave generously to worthy causes, endowed fellowships. He returned.

"I am indeed happier for having shared with others, but the vacancy inside is still there."

"Your division is still addition," said the Wise Man. "And you are not in any sense subtracting." Asking for further explanation, he found the Wise Man busy with other tasks.

"He surely cannot mean that I have to subtract all I have in order to fill the vacancy, but I'll do anything to find inward peace."

"Life is living, not doing, giving, or having," said the Wise Man. "Find Life, and the Giver of Life, and its unfoldment may or may not include doing, giving, or having."

It took many years for the man to comprehend. But he knew that the Wise Man spoke of inward truths, soul growth, and spiritual quest. And his arithmetic improved.

"**M**Y BROTHER and his wife are filled with zeal and enthusiasm about going to the tribe and teaching them, not only the better life of sanitary living, but also their religious concepts. I have tried my best to talk them out of this folly, but they insist that they want to go. Can you talk sense into their heads, Wise Man?"

"The needs of man are many. And this applies equally to your relatives and to the group they desire to visit as missionaries. Your brother and his wife probably need the experience just as much as the recipients of their attention. Since the desire is so strong, and the urgency so compelling, to force a quenching of this flame would be injurious. And, after all, is it not possible that their service can be of considerable good? No, I feel I should not interfere, for I might be disturbing a life pattern necessary for them at this time."

"Well, can't you insist that they prepare themselves more adequately and at least delay their departure?" asked the man. He still held the hope that perhaps the passage of time would serve to squelch their enthusiasm.

The Wise Man said nothing. And the man knew he had his answer.

TWO WOMEN were talking with the Wise Man. One said, "I tried to follow the instructions you gave to my friend in dealing with my son. It worked for her, but it caused confusion in our home. Why?" The Wise Man ignored the question and spoke of other things.

When the visit was ended, the Wise Man said to the women: "Please give me your right shoes." They did, and after a short time, he handed back the shoes, but not to the rightful owner. "Try to wear these now," he said, and then he reached into a small cup and took some seeds which he handed to the women. "Try this new plant in your garden." And they left.

Laboriously they walked down the path, but soon found they had to change their shoes, for both were un-comfortable.

When the seeds were planted, the shady garden produced no plants, while the sunny hillside bloomed with the tiny flowers growing from the seeds.

The woman spoke one day: "I wonder why the Wise Man ignored my question?" And suddenly the two knew they had their answer. The shoes and the seeds!

As a little child, she preferred to play the game of "when I am grown up." At one time it was, "I will be a nurse and heal people." Later it was, "I will be a teacher."

She lived through her teen years, still indulging in future dreams. "I am anxious to establish a library in this town. It will be a building where books for both children and adults will be available. They can study in my library or borrow books for a small fee. This I want to do."

The Wise Man said, "Look, I have a library of books. Here, take them. Use these books and invite people to share the tomes in your home." Her only comment was a surprised, "Now?" Her starry-eyed enthusiasm showed as a scared expression. The Wise Man said, "Go and do."

It soon became known that she had the volumes in her home, and that they were available. Once more the young lady came to visit the Wise Man. "For the first time in my life, I feel that I am living and not dreaming. Frankly, it is a new experience, and I found it uncomfortable at first, but am now delighted. I am grateful to you, oh Wise Man."

But the Wise Man seemingly had not heard, but was busily engaged in cooking a stew.

THE YOUNG man asked:
"Is there a God?"

The Wise Man replied:

"Another's answer to that question is meaningless. You must know for yourself. Approach the question without previous conclusion, in openness and sincerity. For the Source, Allness, Creator, Jehovah, Wisdom, God—call it what you will—is then revealed to you. No life is complete without this, for only this awareness will fill the emptiness of man. It is the path of sanity and comfort, of fulfillment, inward peace, and true happiness.

"Personal awareness and inward verification is most essential. Only the experience that is individual to you will have substance. The details of the revelation may differ greatly from that received by others, but will be suitable to your particular personality and your life situation. You will sense a balance in your activities, and your entire outlook on life will alter and change. It is important that you reserve the possibility that a Higher Power exists and that it is possible to have an intimate relationship with that which you term Divine.''

The young man searched, and found. And they both rejoiced.

The
Wise Man Stories

Early in the morning,
before thoughts and ac-
tivities of the day crowd
into the mind, the Silence
comes.

And into the empty and
quiet mind, the Wise
Man Stories are given.

We call our source by the
name ''Friends.''

Received and Recorded
by
Harold and Alma Smith